garden
dreams and plans

text by h.d.r. campbell

gift

stewart, tabori & chang

For my darling husband, Michael, my partner in gardening, in life, and in love.

Designed by Lisa Vaughn and Melanie Random
Production by Deirdre Duggan

USDA Plant Hardiness Zone Map courtesy of the Agricultural Research Service, USDA.

Published in 1998 and distributed in the U.S. by
Stewart, Tabori & Chang,
a division of U.S. Media Holdings, Inc.
115 West 18th Street, New York, NY 10011

Distributed in Canada by
General Publishing Company Ltd.
30 Lesmill Road
Don Mills, Ontario, Canada M3B 2T6

Sold in Australia by
Peribo Pty. Ltd.
58 Beaumont Road
Mount Kuring-gai, NSW 2080, Australia

Distributed in all other territories by
Grantham Book Services Ltd.
Isaac Newton Way, Alma Park Industrial Estate
Grantham, Lincolnshire, NG31 9SD, England

ISBN: 1-55670-837-8

Printed in China

10 9 8 7 6 5 4 3 2 1

contents

introduction 5

design 7
   the site
   climate conditions
   palette

preparation 29
   the soil

planting 37
   shopping list
   vegetables
   flowers
   flowering vines
   herbs
   fruit
   flowering trees
   roses
   ground covers
   succession planting

care 69
   feeding the garden
   fighting insects & pests
   miscellaneous garden chores
   tools & equipment

harvesting 115
   harvesting shopping list
   canning
   freezing
   drying
   cut flower arrangements
   meals fresh from the garden
   putting the garden to bed
   planting bulbs

birds & butterflies 149

notes & resources 153

man's first home was a garden. Since the Fall, it seems we have been trying to return to Eden in one form or another. Indeed, it is a measure of our spirituality that drives us to create our own gardens - a piece of heaven on earth, our own earthly paradise.

A garden is an expression of you and the vegetation you love. It can be as simple as a row of tulips or as complicated as the Orangerie at Versailles. It can contain vegetables, flowers, herbs, or any combination that the gardener sees fit to grow together. If space is limited, the garden can grow vertically on poles and fences, with curling tendrils vining up and up like Jack's famous beanstalk. Or it can be contained in a single window box with mixed plants of varying heights and hues. In addition to the riot of color and textures, gardens contain secrets which you will be privy to when you harvest your first onion, carrot, radish, or beet, all of which grow under terra firma. A garden can supply one with the sense of place that Virginia Woolf wrote of in *A Room of One's Own*. Fenced or hedged, it is a room of its own; or it can ramble for acres and include ponds and trees and baronial estates.

Begin the garden of your dreams here in this little book. It is filled with tips on the basics that will aid you in your start-up plot. Think about design and site. Then on to soil preparation. Planting the site and installing perhaps a gazing ball or birdbath to it seem as if the garden has been around for more than one season. And caring for your seedlings and tender shoots will put you in a zen frame of mind where you will be transported by the sounds of a humming-bird's wings, no two of which are alike.

design

"to create a garden is to search for a better world"

—*Marina Schinz*

this is where you take a look on paper at your entire site to see exactly what you already have. Get a copy of your property survey and reduce it on a copying machine. Paste it into your planner and draw in walls and other permanent fixtures. On clear acetate or overlay sheets of tracing paper, draw in possible planting areas. Make notes of sun and shade patterns on another overlay. For example, the trees on your property will automatically determine the best spots for shade-loving plants. The setting of your house, whether it is a suburban Tudor on two acres or an apartment building where you have a window box, will dictate different plans according to its relationship to the sun. The decisions you make—to plant flowering shrubs and bushes or sun-loving perennials and low-maintenance herbs—will be guided by what you learn from the overall sketches of the site.

The Detail of Site pages provide space for you to draw the various areas you are developing (the front, back, and sides of your property, for example). Use them to illustrate the specifics; don't forget to include existing out buildings, ponds, et cetera, and to indicate sunny and shady sections.

the site

1/4" = 1 foot in larger area

paste property survey here
then place acetate over survey

the site

1/4" = 1 foot in larger area

paste property survey here
then place acetate over survey

the site

1/4" = 1 foot in larger area

tip *Set your garden with the rows running east to west. Put the shortest plants on the south side and the tallest on the north side to avoid casting unwanted shadows.*

paste property survey here
then place acetate over survey

the site

paste property survey here
then place acetate over survey

detail of site
1/2" = 1 foot in smaller areas

paste property survey here
then place acetate over survey

detail of site

1/2" = 1 foot in smaller areas

paste property survey here
then place acetate over survey

detail of site

1/2" = 1 foot in smaller areas

paste property survey here
then place acetate over survey

detail of site
1/2" = 1 foot in smaller areas

paste property survey here
then place acetate over survey

site notes

One rule of thumb in assessing what will grow with best results in your garden is simple: Look around at neighboring sites. The vegetation that is happiest will be readily apparent. Talk to other local gardeners, who, more often than not, will love to share their experiences and trade seeds, cuttings, and gardening tips with you. Pay attention to the weather. In the northeast, gardeners strive to plant after all danger of frost has passed, while in the desert, plants that need plentiful rainfall are to be avoided. The hardiness zone map will help you to choose the plants that thrive in your part of the country. Growing plants suited to the conditions of your site will make you nature's compatible partner.

usda plant hardiness zone map

RANGE OF AVERAGE ANNUAL MINIMUM
TEMPERATURES FOR EACH ZONE

ZONE 1	BELOW -50°F	
ZONE 2	-50° TO -40°	
ZONE 3	-40° TO -30°	
ZONE 4	-30° TO -20°	
ZONE 5	-20° TO -10°	
ZONE 6	-10° TO 0°	
ZONE 7	0° TO 10°	
ZONE 8	10° TO 20°	
ZONE 9	20° TO 30°	
ZONE 10	30° TO 40°	
ZONE 11	ABOVE 40°	

climate notes

	temperature a.m.	temperature p.m.
date/planted/site:	sun:	sun:
	shade:	shade:
date/planted/site:	sun:	sun:
	shade:	shade:
date/planted/site:	sun:	sun:
	shade:	shade:
date/planted/site:	sun:	sun:
	shade:	shade:
date/planted/site:	sun:	sun:
	shade:	shade:
date/planted/site:	sun:	sun:
	shade:	shade:
date/planted/site:	sun:	sun:
	shade:	shade:
date/planted/site:	sun:	sun:
	shade:	shade:

notes:

tip *Contact your local cooperative extension service for statistics on your area. Expected freeze dates and annual rain-fall reports can be very useful while planning your garden.*

climate notes

	temperature a.m.	temperature p.m.
date/planted/site:	sun:	sun:
	shade:	shade:
date/planted/site:	sun:	sun:
	shade:	shade:
date/planted/site:	sun:	sun:
	shade:	shade:
date/planted/site:	sun:	sun:
	shade:	shade:
date/planted/site:	sun:	sun:
	shade:	shade:
date/planted/site:	sun:	sun:
	shade:	shade:
date/planted/site:	sun:	sun:
	shade:	shade:
date/planted/site:	sun:	sun:
	shade:	shade:
date/planted/site:	sun:	sun:
	shade:	shade:
date/planted/site:	sun:	sun:
	shade:	shade:

climate notes

	temperature a.m.	temperature p.m.
date/planted/site:	sun:	sun:
	shade:	shade:
date/planted/site:	sun:	sun:
	shade:	shade:
date/planted/site:	sun:	sun:
	shade:	shade:
date/planted/site:	sun:	sun:
	shade:	shade:
date/planted/site:	sun:	sun:
	shade:	shade:
date/planted/site:	sun:	sun:
	shade:	shade:
date/planted/site:	sun:	sun:
	shade:	shade:
date/planted/site:	sun:	sun:
	shade:	shade:

notes:

tip *A full-grown plant will more than likely be one-half to two-thirds as wide as it is tall. The height of plants is indicated on seed packages and in catalogs.*

climate notes

	temperature a.m.	temperature p.m.
date/planted/site:	sun:	sun:
	shade:	shade:
date/planted/site:	sun:	sun:
	shade:	shade:
date/planted/site:	sun:	sun:
	shade:	shade:
date/planted/site:	sun:	sun:
	shade:	shade:
date/planted/site:	sun:	sun:
	shade:	shade:
date/planted/site:	sun:	sun:
	shade:	shade:
date/planted/site:	sun:	sun:
	shade:	shade:
date/planted/site:	sun:	sun:
	shade:	shade:
date/planted/site:	sun:	sun:
	shade:	shade:

climate notes

in keeping with the drawings you did in the earlier pages, think about color as you prepare to plant. Gardeners often refer to warm and cool colors and warn against mixing them. I prefer to think in terms of pastels and brights. On occasion a single color can be used to stunning effect, as in the white gardens at Sissinghurst.

Experiment with colored pencils or pastels by smudging combinations of colors together in groups on the pages. See how different colors actually look when placed side by side. Notice how in nature the colors always seem perfectly combined. Consider an apple tree in bloom: the buds are pink and open up to a pale cream color tinged with pink contrasted by soft green leaves. Using colored pencils or pastels to illustrate the trees, shrubs, flowers, and vegetables you envision will aid you in visualizing your garden before you plant.

palette

palette

palette

preparation

"what makes a garden? and why do gardens grow? love lives in gardens —god and lovers know!"

—Carolyn Giltinan

Soil varies from region to

region and almost everyone adjusts it according to their own desires. Take the squeeze test! It is easy to see if your soil is workable in the spring. Just hold a handful of dirt in your hand. Squeeze it into a ball. Open your hand. If the ball sticks together, it is too wet to work. If it crumbles when you open your hand, it is ready to be worked.

There are numerous additives and organic materials you can use to achieve friability, that perfect soil texture for germinating seeds and growing seedlings. In addition, the pH value of the soil (indicating degrees of alkalinity or acidity) can be moderately adjusted to suit your plants. The shortcut pH test: Take a few spoonfuls of dry soil and put them into a jar with an equal amount of white vinegar. Close the jar and shake. Open the jar and listen carefully. If there is a loud fizzling noise, the soil is very alkaline. If there is only a faint fizzing noise, it is only a bit alkaline.

Use the following pages to record the original soil conditions and the improvements you make. Record the pH of your soil before and after you adjust it; test it again in two weeks for a more long-term reading. Then add earthworms; their travels will break down the organic matter and aerate the soil.

soil texture chart

	before	treatment	results
date:			
site:			
soil condition:			
date:			
site:			
soil condition:			
date:			
site:			
soil condition:			
date:			
site:			
soil condition:			
date:			
site:			
soil condition:			

notes:

tip *Good drainage is of primary importance. Don't ever plant in soggy soil; there won't be enough oxygen in the soil for healthy plants to grow. Also, avoid cold pockets—for example, at the base of a hill—where it can frost easily.*

pH balance chart

	before	treatment	results
date:			
site:			
soil condition:			
date:			
site:			
soil condition:			
date:			
site:			
soil condition:			
date:			
site:			
soil condition:			
date:			
site:			
soil condition:			
date:			
site:			
soil condition:			

soil texture chart

	before	treatment	results
date:			
site:			
soil condition:			
date:			
site:			
soil condition:			
date:			
site:			
soil condition:			
date:			
site:			
soil condition:			
date:			
site:			
soil condition:			
date:			
site:			
soil condition:			

pH balance chart

	before	treatment	results
date:			
site:			
soil condition:			
date:			
site:			
soil condition:			
date:			
site:			
soil condition:			
date:			
site:			
soil condition:			
date:			
site:			
soil condition:			

notes:

tip *A pH between 5.7 and 6.7 is ideal for growing most plants. Above 6.7 it is too alkaline and below 5.7 is too acidic. In my garden, the soil is quite acidic, so I do not adjust the pH where my acid-loving blueberry bush is growing and it seems very happy.*

soil notes

soil notes

soil notes

planting

"those who labor in the earth are the chosen people of god."

—Thomas Jefferson

the following pages will serve as a shopping list for your vegetable, flower, and herb gardens. Merely circle the seeds you wish to order in one color and the seedlings you wish to purchase in another and you will find yourself with an organized list. Record the particular variety and later the results. Of course, you will circle your old favorites; I encourage you to try some new varieties too.

vegetable	variety	result
arugula		
asparagus		
beet		
black-eyed pea		
broccoli		
broccoli rabe		
brussels sprout		

vegetables

vegetable	variety	result
bush lima bean		
butter bean		
cabbage		
carrot		
cauliflower		
cherry tomato		
cranberry bean		
cucumber		
oriental cucumber		
eggplant		
endive		
garlic		

vegetables

vegetable	variety	result
gourd		
hot & sweet pepper		
jerusalem artichoke		
kale		
leek		
lettuce		
mesclun		
new potato		
okra		
onion		
pea		
peanut		

vegetables

vegetable	variety	result
plum tomato		
pole snap bean		
potato		
pumpkin		
radicchio		
radish		
rhubarb		
shallot		
snap bean		
snow pea		
spinach		
squash		

vegetables

vegetable	variety	result
sweet peppers		
sweet potato		
swiss chard		
tomatillo		
tomato		
turnip		
zucchini		
other		

vegetables

vegetable	variety	result
other		

perennials	variety	result
achillea		
balloon flower		
bellflower		
bleeding heart		
buddleia		
columbine		
coneflower		
coralbell		
coreopsis		
day lily		
delphinium		
dianthus		

flowers/perennials

perennials	variety	result
euphorbia		
ferns		
foxglove		
geranium		
heliopsis, ballerina		
hibiscus		
hollyhock		
hosta		
iris		
loosestrife		
monkshood		
peony		

flowers/perennials

perennials	variety	result
phlox		
pink		
primrose		
rudbeckia		
russell lupine		
scabiosa		
sea lavender		
sedum		
shasta daisy		
veronica		
other		

45

perennials	variety	result
other		

flowers/annuals

annuals	variety	result
aster		
bells of ireland		
black-eyed susan		
calendula		
cazania		
celosia		
cleome		
clianthus		
cosmos		
flowering cabbage		
flowering kale		
forget-me-not		

flowers/annuals

annuals	variety	result
four-o'clock		
gloriosa daisy		
helichrysum		
ice plant		
other		

flowering vines

vine	variety	result
cardinal climber		
clematis		
dwarf morning glory		
honeysuckle		
moonflower		
morning glory		
trumpet creeper		
wisteria		
other		

herbs

herb	variety	result
angelica		
basil		
bay		
bergamot		
borage		
calendula		
catnip		
chamomile		
chive		
coriander		
dill		
fennel		

herbs

herb	variety	result
horseradish		
lady's mantle		
lamb's ear		
lavender		
lemon balm		
lemon verbena		
marjoram		
mint		
mullein		
oregano		
parsley		
rosemary		

herbs

herb	variety	result
rue		
sage		
santolina		
savory		
tarragon		
thyme		
valerian		
yarrow		
other		

herbs

herb	variety	result
other		

fruit

fruit	variety	result
apple		
blueberry		
blackberry		
currant		
fig		
gooseberry		
grape, seedless		
kiwi		
peach		
pear		
persimmon		
plum		

fruit

fruit	variety	result
strawberry		
raspberry		
other		

55

flowering trees

tree	variety	result
crabapple		
dogwood		
golden chain		
magnolia		
mimosa		
myrtle		
redbud		
rose		
tree hydrangea		
tree wisteria		
other		

flowering trees

tree	variety	result
other		

ground covers

ground cover	variety	result
crown vetch		
english ivy		
irish moss		
lily of the valley		
pachysandra		
periwinkle		
other		

easy to grow in full sun with the correct conditions, roses are a hardy though picky lot. Choose the ones that grow best in your climate and respect their needs. Hybrids need to be somewhat pampered. Floribundas are more disease-resistant than hybrids and, with their short, stocky stature can play a role in landscaping your property. If you have lots of room, grandifloras may be a better fit. I adore climbing roses and window gardeners may wish to cultivate miniature roses.

The ideal spot should be prepared in the fall and planted the following spring. If you haven't grown roses before, invest in a book that devotes a lot of attention to them. Advance information can spare you from losing your precious plants to inferior care or disease. Reading up on the various diseases and pests roses are prone to will enable you to deal with them specifically. Refer to books with illustrations of the potential problems so you will be able to recognize them. Blackspot (mildew), rust, rose canker, and aphids all inflict damage in different ways and leave individual telltale signs on the leaves.

roses

the workspace for roses is rather detailed and a little more complicated than other recordkeeping spaces in this book. I have constructed this to accommodate those whose passion is roses. These intrepid souls already know how detailed the care of these prickly stemmed shrubs can be. The Where Purchased column is particularly

type	where purchased	date planted

roses

practical as an easy reference should returns or replacements be necessary.
Charts with dates to fill in when you plant and when you prune and dead-
head will keep you on track in caring for your roses. Don't forget the first
step in winter protection: Water well. Roses need moisture on their roots
during the frozen winter months.

pruning/deadheading	pest/disease control	winter protection

type	where purchased	date planted

notes:

tip *A soaker hose can be invaluable for watering roses. This method keeps moisture away from the leaves and decreases the possibility of disease.*

roses

pruning/deadheading	pest/disease control	winter protection

rose notes

succession planting

o ensure continuous harvest, succession planting is ideal. Using the charts provided, keep track of the name of the plant, the date you planted, the actual pull date (for vegetables) and remind yourself when to replant.

plant	date planted	pull date	replant date

succession planting

plant	date planted	pull date	replant date

succession planting

plant	date planted	pull date	replant date

succession planting

plant	date planted	pull date	replant date

notes:

tip _Use plants that require various planting depths. In the Fall, plant Spring bulbs. Perennials that bloom later can be planted a few inches above the bulbs._

care

"a **weed** is no more than a **flower** in disguise, which is **seen** through at once, if love give **man eyes**"

—*James Russell Lowell*

after the superb preparation you have no doubt
completed by now, it would be a shame were you not to commit to
caring for your garden. Actually, this working in the soil, this
getting your hands dirty, this intimate connection with your plants
is what gardeners enjoy the most. How perfectly wonderful to coax
those little seedlings along to become strong, vibrant plants. How
satisfying to clear out the weeds that threaten them and create nice
clean rows. Protecting them from predators and giving them what
they need to thrive is a parental kind of behavior. It is no accident
that gardeners are nurturers. Or are nurturers gardeners?

The fertilizing of your garden can be recorded in monthly
calendars. In the vegetable garden or when treating fruit trees or
berry bushes (or anything that is edible, including certain flowers),
be sure to use only organic products to safeguard your family's
health.

notes

recording when you sprayed your apple trees
for gypsy moths or used Bt on your tomatoes to combat tomato
hornworms will make it easier to keep track of when to repeat
treatments. You might also want to note the product you used.
I like to experiment with organic products and record how well
they worked. Too bad the slug traps didn't work. The deer drank
the beer in the traps and tossed them out of the pansy bed.
What a party!

january

monday	tuesday	wednesday	thursday	friday	saturday	sunday

january

monday	tuesday	wednesday	thursday	friday	saturday	sunday

february

monday	tuesday	wednesday	thursday	friday	saturday	sunday

february

monday	tuesday	wednesday	thursday	friday	saturday	sunday

march

monday	tuesday	wednesday	thursday	friday	saturday	sunday

march

monday	tuesday	wednesday	thursday	friday	saturday	sunday

april

monday	tuesday	wednesday	thursday	friday	saturday	sunday

april

monday	tuesday	wednesday	thursday	friday	saturday	sunday

april

monday	tuesday	wednesday	thursday	friday	saturday	sunday

monday	tuesday	wednesday	thursday	friday	saturday	sunday

may

monday	tuesday	wednesday	thursday	friday	saturday	sunday

may

monday	tuesday	wednesday	thursday	friday	saturday	sunday

may

monday	tuesday	wednesday	thursday	friday	saturday	sunday

may

monday	tuesday	wednesday	thursday	friday	saturday	sunday

june

monday	tuesday	wednesday	thursday	friday	saturday	sunday

june

monday	tuesday	wednesday	thursday	friday	saturday	sunday

june

monday	tuesday	wednesday	thursday	friday	saturday	sunday

june

monday	tuesday	wednesday	thursday	friday	saturday	sunday

july

monday	tuesday	wednesday	thursday	friday	saturday	sunday

july

monday	tuesday	wednesday	thursday	friday	saturday	sunday

july

monday	tuesday	wednesday	thursday	friday	saturday	sunday

july

monday	tuesday	wednesday	thursday	friday	saturday	sunday

august

monday	tuesday	wednesday	thursday	friday	saturday	sunday

august

monday	tuesday	wednesday	thursday	friday	saturday	sunday

august

monday	tuesday	wednesday	thursday	friday	saturday	sunday

august

monday	tuesday	wednesday	thursday	friday	saturday	sunday

september

monday	tuesday	wednesday	thursday	friday	saturday	sunday

september

monday	tuesday	wednesday	thursday	friday	saturday	sunday

september

monday	tuesday	wednesday	thursday	friday	saturday	sunday

september

monday	tuesday	wednesday	thursday	friday	saturday	sunday

october

monday	tuesday	wednesday	thursday	friday	saturday	sunday

october

monday	tuesday	wednesday	thursday	friday	saturday	sunday

november

monday	tuesday	wednesday	thursday	friday	saturday	sunday

november

monday	tuesday	wednesday	thursday	friday	saturday	sunday

december

monday	tuesday	wednesday	thursday	friday	saturday	sunday

december

monday	tuesday	wednesday	thursday	friday	saturday	sunday

notes

how often you perform the following garden chores is up to you and will be determined on site from your own observations. This checklist is just a tool to make it easier for you to focus on the minutiae that signal the difference between a good garden and a great garden.

- [ ] cultivating
- [ ] cutting back
- [ ] deadheading
- [ ] mulching
- [ ] pinching
- [ ] thinning
- [ ] tying
- [ ] spraying
- [ ] staking
- [ ] watering
- [ ] weeding

miscellaneous garden chore notes

date   *date*

We all have our favorite tools, clothing, and equipment, but that doesn't stop us from adding to our collection. Following is a checklist of things you may want to invest in this season. If you purchase a large item like a rototiller, check it off here. On the following pages, note the year of purchase and length of warranty.

- ☐ Avon Skin So Soft (a great insect repellent)
- ☐ bucket
- ☐ dibble
- ☐ drinking water
- ☐ edger shovel
- ☐ garden hose
- ☐ good gardening gloves
- ☐ hedge trimmers
- ☐ hoe
- ☐ hose hanger or reel
- ☐ kneeling pad
- ☐ peony rings
- ☐ pruning shears
- ☐ rake
- ☐ rototiller
- ☐ shovel

- ☐ sprinkler
- ☐ string or twine
- ☐ sun hat
- ☐ sunblock
- ☐ tomato cones
- ☐ trowel
- ☐ watering can
- ☐ wellies
- ☐ wheelbarrow
- ☐ small stakes four to six feet in height
- ☐ other

_____
_____
_____

tools & equipment

tool: _____ date acquired: _____

warranty & service contract: _____

_____

_____

tool: _____ date acquired: _____

warranty & service contract: _____

_____

_____

tool: _____ date acquired: _____

warranty & service contract: _____

_____

_____

tool: _____ date acquired: _____

warranty & service contract: _____

_____

_____

tool: _____ date acquired: _____

warranty & service contract: _____

_____

_____

tool: _____ date acquired: _____

warranty & service contract: _____

_____

_____

tool: _____ date acquired: _____

warranty & service contract: _____

_____

_____

tool: _____ date acquired: _____

warranty & service contract: _____

_____

_____

tool: _____ date acquired: _____

warranty & service contract: _____

_____

_____

tool: _____ date acquired: _____

warranty & service contract: _____

_____

_____

tool: _____ date acquired: _____

warranty & service contract: _____

_____

_____

notes:

tip _Clean your tools and oil their metal parts to avoid rust, especially the ones you left out in the rain. Before storing for the winter, sharpen them so they will be ready to use come spring._

tools & equipment notes

harvesting

"wouldn't the world be a horrible place without garlic?"

—*Michael Campbell*

enjoy the beautiful flowers, delicious vegetables, and delightful views in your garden. Transform them for winter use with the preservation method of your choice. There are a variety of ways to store or "put up" your organic treasures. Canning, once the most popular way to keep perishables, is still a useful and decorative means to store food for the coming months. It is time-consuming, but can be fun and a satisfying experience. Freezing, a more modern approach, is quick and easy and not that tricky. It is the modern cook's time-saving answer. (The tips below will aid you in retaining the most flavor in your frozen goodies). Drying is a good bet for the more aromatic of your herbs and can be accomplished with a minimum of trouble. Dried flowers become enchanted objects that will last for months and need little or no maintenance. Any one of the above methods will help you to enjoy the bounty of your garden long past summer.

On the next page, make a shopping list of canning equipment and recipe ingredients, etc.

shopping list

canning

Record how many pints of bread-and-butter pickles or quarts of stewed tomatoes you put up, or pots of raspberry jam you made from your own garden! You will love comparing from year to year. If you have not canned before, use the shopping list space provided. Canning requires its own equipment. Consult *The Joy of Cooking* for the best advice on supplies and methods.

canned goods:	size:	quantity:	date finished:
notes:			

canned goods:	size:	quantity:	date finished:
notes:			

canned goods:	size:	quantity:	date finished:
notes:			

canned goods:	size:	quantity:	date finished:
notes:			

canned goods:	size:	quantity:	date finished:
notes:			

canning

canned goods:	size:	quantity:	date finished:
notes:			

canned goods:	size:	quantity:	date finished:
notes:			

canned goods:	size:	quantity:	date finished:
notes:			

canned goods:	size:	quantity:	date finished:
notes:			

canned goods:	size:	quantity:	date finished:
notes:			

canned goods:	size:	quantity:	date finished:
notes:			

canned goods:	size:	quantity:	date finished:
notes:			

canned goods:	size:	quantity:	date finished:
notes:			

canned goods:	size:	quantity:	date finished:
notes:			

canning

canned goods: size: quantity: date finished:

notes:

---

canned goods: size: quantity: date finished:

notes:

---

canned goods: size: quantity: date finished:

notes:

---

canned goods: size: quantity: date finished:

notes:

---

canned goods: size: quantity: date finished:

notes:

---

canned goods: size: quantity: date finished:

notes:

---

canned goods: size: quantity: date finished:

notes:

---

canned goods: size: quantity: date finished:

notes:

---

canned goods: size: quantity: date finished:

notes:

canning notes

freezing

While frozen goods aren't as exciting to look at as those jars of canned goods lined up on a pantry shelf, you will still get a major kick out of eating homegrown vegetables from the freezer in midwinter. Keep track of how many bags of butter beans you froze or how many ears of corn you put up. Record when you open the last jar or freezer bag to compare how far into the winter you enjoyed the harvest. My favorite easy thing to freeze is blueberries for pancakes.

frozen item:	quantity:	date frozen:	date finished:
notes:			

frozen item:	quantity:	date frozen:	date finished:
notes:			

frozen item:	quantity:	date frozen:	date finished:
notes:			

frozen item:	quantity:	date frozen:	date finished:
notes:			

frozen item:	quantity:	date frozen:	date finished:
notes:			

freezing

frozen item: _____ quantity: _____ date frozen: _____ date finished: _____

notes: _____

frozen item: _____ quantity: _____ date frozen: _____ date finished: _____

notes: _____

frozen item: _____ quantity: _____ date frozen: _____ date finished: _____

notes: _____

frozen item: _____ quantity: _____ date frozen: _____ date finished: _____

notes: _____

frozen item: _____ quantity: _____ date frozen: _____ date finished: _____

notes: _____

frozen item: _____ quantity: _____ date frozen: _____ date finished: _____

notes: _____

frozen item: _____ quantity: _____ date frozen: _____ date finished: _____

notes: _____

miscellaneous notes:

tip *Speak to your county agricultural agent about what freezes well.*

freezing notes

tip *The first of any crop keeps its flavor best.*

i like to dry herbs and flowers for winter use
rather than using expensive commercially prepared products.
Many herbs and flowers readily lend themselves to this easy
process. Every winter, my dining room centerpiece is a huge
bouquet of dried hydrangeas.

Herbs

Pick your herbs on a clear day just after the dew has dissipated.
They should be picked just before they flower. The best environment
for drying herbs is a room with good air circulation. Tie them
together in small bunches and hang them upside down. Allow them
to dry for about two weeks. Check them to be sure they are
uniformly dry before storing in glass jars. If the weather is damp,
try drying your herbs in the oven on a cookie sheet at the lowest
temperature possible. Crack the oven door a bit to allow moisture
to escape.

herbs

herbs:	date picked:	result:
notes:		

herbs:	date picked:	result:
notes:		

herbs:	date picked:	result:
notes:		

herbs:	date picked:	result:
notes:		

herbs:	date picked:	result:
notes:		

herbs:	date picked:	result:
notes:		

herbs:	date picked:	result:
notes:		

miscellaneous notes:

secret *The more aromatic the herb in its original state, the more aromatic it will be in its dried state. Sage, bay leaves, rosemary, and thyme are good drying choices.*

herbs

herbs: date picked: result:

notes:

herbs: date picked: result:

notes:

herbs: date picked: result:

notes:

herbs: date picked: result:

notes:

herbs: date picked: result:

notes:

herbs: date picked: result:

notes:

herbs: date picked: result:

notes:

herbs: date picked: result:

notes:

herb drying notes

dried flowers

Pick flowers just before their peak, a whisper before their full bloom. Keep them in a dry place away from direct sunlight. Bunch them as you do for your herbs and dry upside down. Flowers require more time to dry than herbs. Give them at least a month of drying time and check on them during the drying period. I like to recall how I used them and have provided a space for you to do the same.

flower	when picked	how used

jot down the flowers you use in your arrangements.

Mix wildflowers with cultivated ones for a casual and informal appearance. Or make simplicity your theme: a bouquet can be all one flower, such as pansies in a bud vase or Queen Anne's Lace in a fruit jar. I like to use cut flowers tied into the ribbon of a gift-wrapped package. They are more beautiful than floral wrapping paper. Keep your arrangements out of direct sunlight and they will last longer.

flower	how used

cut flower arrangements

flower	how used

these notes are among my favorites to keep.
As eating trends change and the seasons pass, it is easy to forget the
delicious mesclun salad with yellow tomatoes or the grilled eggplant
or steamed baby beets that you ate all summer long. Your records
will enable you to replicate this year's garden menu whenever you
wish. It's fun, too, to record the event for which you made a favorite
dish, no matter if it was for a very important guest or for lunch all
by yourself.

dish:	date:	occasion:
notes:		

dish:	date:	occasion:
notes:		

dish:	date:	occasion:
notes:		

dish:	date:	occasion:
notes:		

dish:	date:	occasion:
notes:		

meals fresh from the garden

dish: _____ date: _____ occasion: _____
notes: _____

dish: _____ date: _____ occasion: _____
notes: _____

dish: _____ date: _____ occasion: _____
notes: _____

dish: _____ date: _____ occasion: _____
notes: _____

dish: _____ date: _____ occasion: _____
notes: _____

dish: _____ date: _____ occasion: _____
notes: _____

dish: _____ date: _____ occasion: _____
notes: _____

dish: _____ date: _____ occasion: _____
notes: _____

dish: _____ date: _____ occasion: _____
notes: _____

recipes

recipes

recipes

recipes

even the most casual of gardeners knows that if you take the time to "clean house" in your garden at the end of the growing season, it will be much easier to rework the soil and begin again next year. Tidying up the garden at season's end will discourage unwanted pests and insects as well.

As you spruce up your plot and clear away the spent flowers stalks of the delphinium and the brown leaves on the iris, you have optioned a space to plant spring bulbs. Those crisp fall days are the perfect time to ensure your garden's early start. After working my gardens in Pennsylvania for ten years, I know that daffodils, hyacinths and grape hyacinths, will return year after year. Alas, tulips, a flower I dearly treasure, are the chipmunks' favorite dinner. Plant bulbs for a few years and you will come to know which ones will grace your plot annually while you marvel at the profusion of those colorful blooms that mark spring in the garden.

task: date completed:

_____   _____

_____   _____

_____   _____

_____   _____

_____   _____

_____   _____

_____   _____

_____   _____

_____   _____

_____   _____

_____   _____

_____   _____

_____   _____

_____   _____

_____   _____

_____   _____

_____   _____

_____   _____

task: date completed:

_____   _____

_____   _____

_____   _____

_____   _____

_____   _____

_____   _____

_____   _____

_____   _____

_____   _____

_____   _____

_____   _____

_____   _____

_____   _____

_____   _____

_____   _____

_____   _____

_____   _____

_____   _____

_____   _____

_____   _____

_____   _____

_____   _____

_____   _____

putting the garden to bed

task: date completed:

_____   _____

_____   _____

_____   _____

_____   _____

_____   _____

_____   _____

_____   _____

_____   _____

_____   _____

_____   _____

_____   _____

_____   _____

_____   _____

_____   _____

notes:

tip _This is the time to collect seeds from your favorite flowers. If the seeds seem very loose as if they will drop off easily, place newspaper under the plant and then gingerly cut the stem of the plant whose seeds you wish to capture. Softly shake the seeds onto the paper. Store in small envelopes that you label and keep in a cool, dry place._

planting bulbs

bulb:	date planted:
how fed:	date of bloom:
notes:	

bulb:	date planted:
how fed:	date of bloom:
notes:	

bulb:	date planted:
how fed:	date of bloom:
notes:	

bulb:	date planted:
how fed:	date of bloom:
notes:	

bulb:	date planted:
how fed:	date of bloom:
notes:	

bulb:	date planted:
how fed:	date of bloom:
notes:	

bulb:	date planted:
how fed:	date of bloom:
notes:	

bulb:	date planted:
how fed:	date of bloom:
notes:	

planting bulbs

bulb: _____   date planted: _____
how fed: _____   date of bloom: _____
notes: _____

bulb: _____   date planted: _____
how fed: _____   date of bloom: _____
notes: _____

bulb: _____   date planted: _____
how fed: _____   date of bloom: _____
notes: _____

bulb: _____   date planted: _____
how fed: _____   date of bloom: _____
notes: _____

bulb: _____   date planted: _____
how fed: _____   date of bloom: _____
notes: _____

bulb: _____   date planted: _____
how fed: _____   date of bloom: _____
notes: _____

bulb: _____   date planted: _____
how fed: _____   date of bloom: _____
notes: _____

bulb: _____   date planted: _____
how fed: _____   date of bloom: _____
notes: _____

bulbs planting notes

birds & butterflies

"birds are like children, easy to love and easy to spoil."

—*Anonymous*

i love birdsong so much that I have an audio tape of songbirds to play all winter long when many of the singers have flown south. In addition to their glorious melodies, birds offer many benefits. They can eat thousands of insects daily and spread seeds throughout their travels. And how magical to have creatures that can fly right there in your own garden. Butterflies, those delicate multihued winged fantasies, add a fanciful note while pollinating gardens. Though it doesn't look it, they work as hard as bees.

It is not uncommon to note more than 100 species of birds in one's own backyard over the course of a year. Birders record their observations each year for comparison with other years. Record your sightings of the first of the varying butterfly species, as well.

birds & butterflies

species: _____ date first seen: _____

notes: _____

species: _____ date first seen: _____

notes: _____

species: _____ date first seen: _____

notes: _____

species: _____ date first seen: _____

notes: _____

species: _____ date first seen: _____

notes: _____

species: _____ date first seen: _____

notes: _____

species: _____ date first seen: _____

notes: _____

species: _____ date first seen: _____

notes: _____

species: _____ date first seen: _____

notes: _____

species: _____ date first seen: _____

notes: _____

species: _____ date first seen: _____

notes: _____

species: _____ date first seen: _____

notes: _____

species: _____ date first seen: _____

notes: _____

species: _____ date first seen: _____

notes: _____

bird & butterfly notes

notes&resources

"the love of gardening is a seed that once sown never dies"

—*Gertrude Jekyll*

notes & resources

i find keeping a record of how things did, what worked well, and what never to try growing again to be enormously useful. Your notes, compiled year after gardening year, will aid you in improving the problem areas in your garden and give you a record of your brilliant successes. Often, after working a site all summer long, I have a brainstorm about what would be wonderful to include in next year's garden. One year, I noted that an arch over the entrance to the vegetable garden would be a good idea. The following summer, I had an arch completely covered in Heavenly Blue morning glories.

It's also invaluable to keep a personal record of the companies and people who provide services: the people I call for a truckload of cow manure, the man who mows the lawn, the Burpee garden information hot line, and the local nurseries I patronize.

notes

site: _____   note: _____

site: _____   note: _____

site: _____   note: _____

site: _____   note: _____

site: _____   note: _____

site: _____   note: _____

site: _____   note: _____

notes

site: _____

note: _____
_____

site: _____

note: _____
_____

site: _____

note: _____
_____

site: _____

note: _____
_____
_____

site: _____

note: _____
_____

site: _____

note: _____
_____

site: _____

note: _____
_____

site: _____

note: _____
_____

resources

service:

name:

address:

phone number:

fax:

e-mail:

notes:

service:

name:

address:

phone number:

fax:

e-mail:

notes:

service:

name:

address:

phone number:

fax:

e-mail:

notes:

service:

name:

address:

phone number:

fax:

e-mail:

notes:

resources

service: _____

name: _____

address: _____

_____

phone number: _____

fax: _____

e-mail: _____

notes: _____

_____

_____

_____

service: _____

name: _____

address: _____

_____

phone number: _____

fax: _____

e-mail: _____

notes: _____

_____

_____

_____

service: _____

name: _____

address: _____

_____

phone number: _____

fax: _____

e-mail: _____

notes: _____

_____

_____

service: _____

name: _____

address: _____

_____

phone number: _____

fax: _____

e-mail: _____

notes: _____

_____

_____

resources

service: _____   service: _____

name: _____   name: _____

address: _____   address: _____

_____   _____

phone number: _____   phone number: _____

fax: _____   fax: _____

e-mail: _____   e-mail: _____

notes: _____   notes: _____

_____   _____

_____   _____

_____   _____

---

service: _____   service: _____

name: _____   name: _____

address: _____   address: _____

_____   _____

phone number: _____   phone number: _____

fax: _____   fax: _____

e-mail: _____   e-mail: _____

notes: _____   notes: _____

_____   _____

_____   _____

_____   _____

resources

service: _____

name: _____

address: _____

_____

_____

phone number: _____

fax: _____

e-mail: _____

notes: _____

_____

_____

_____

service: _____

name: _____

address: _____

_____

_____

phone number: _____

fax: _____

e-mail: _____

notes: _____

_____

_____

_____

service: _____

name: _____

address: _____

_____

_____

phone number: _____

fax: _____

e-mail: _____

notes: _____

_____

_____

_____

service: _____

name: _____

address: _____

_____

_____

phone number: _____

fax: _____

e-mail: _____

notes: _____

_____

_____

_____

notes